TOP TENS

EXTREME MACHINES

No. 9 V-22 Osprey Tiltrotor

Copyright © ticktock Entertainment Ltd 2005
First published in Great Britain in 2005 by ticktock Media Ltd,
Unit 2, Orchard Business Centre, North Farm Road, Tunbridge Wells, Kent TN2 3XF
ISBN 1 86007 915 6 pbk
Printed in China
A CIP catalogue record for this book is available from the British Library.

All rights reserved. No part of this publication may be reproduced, copied, stored in a retrieval system or transmitted in any form or by any means electronic, mechanical, photocopying, recording or otherwise without prior written permission of the copyright owner.

Picture credits (t=top; b=bottom; c=centre; l=left; r=right): Alvey and Towers: 8-9 all, 10-11 all, 12-13 all, 14-15 all, 18-19 all. Aviation Picture Library: 26b. Corbis: 22-23 all, 24-25 all. Fast Car Photo Library: 27 all. JAMSTEC: 6-7 all. NASA: 16-17 all, 20-21 all. Water Sports Photo Library: 26t.

Every effort has been made to trace the copyright holders, and we apologise in advance for any unintentional omissions. We would be pleased to insert the appropriate acknowledgements in any subsequent edition of this publication.

CONTENTS

Machines of all kinds make our lives easier. The earliest machine may have been a simple counting frame. Later, machines were developed to help with jobs like harvesting crops. When the engine was invented, machines began to be linked with power and size. The bigger, faster, more powerful and more expensive something is, the more notice people seem to take. This book presents our Top Ten of the most extreme machines, rated according to:

SPEED

For this category, we looked at the top speed of the machine. This is not always the most important thing; it could be that the machine does not really need to go fast. In other cases, especially when machines were developed to break records, speed is definitely one of the most important factors. There are a lot of record-breakers in this book!

NO.7 — THRUST SSC

Thrust SSC (Supersonic Car) is the fastest and most powerful car ever built. British designer Richard Noble built the car to break the sound barrier over land. On October 15, 1997, at Black Rock Desert, Nevada, US it reached the record-breaking speed of 1,232 km/h. It was driven by RAF pilot Andy Green.

SPEED
Thrust's top speed is 850 mph, and it can go from 0-160 km/h in 4 seconds. It **accelerated** to 965 km/h in just 6 seconds.

FEATURES
The driver enters by opening a roof hatch. The vehicle is as powerful as 145 Formula One racing cars, or 1,000 Ford Escorts.

Thrust SSC was the first car to break the sound barrier.

SIZE
Thrust weighs 9 tonnes, and a parachute braking system is used to slow it down safely.

12

FEATURES

This is the category in which we look at the practical details. We have also tried to include the most interesting things we could find out about the machine. Which extreme machine is as powerful as 1,000 Ford Escorts? Which was made using more than a billion parts? The answers are in this book.

SIZE

Many of the machines we chose are the biggest of their type in the world. For others, size is not the most important factor, and the machine is only as big as it needs to be to do its job.

POWER

This section looks at how the machine works, and how powerful it is. This measurement is often given in **horsepower**. If a machine is described as 1,000 horsepower, it is as powerful as 1,000 horses would be. We also include details such as the type of engine and the fuel used.

VALUE

This category is all about how much it costs to develop the machine, and whether it was worth the money. When a machine has been built only to break a record, it is difficult to work out what it is worth. If the machine also has some practical purpose, it is easier to make a judgment about its value.

This record-breaking car draws crowds whenever it is on display.

EXTREME SCORES

Supersonic speed and incredible power makes Thrust SSC a really extreme machine.

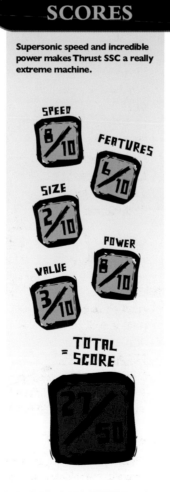

SPEED 8/10

FEATURES 6/10

SIZE 2/10

POWER 8/10

VALUE 3/10

= TOTAL SCORE

27/50

POWER
Its two Rolls Royce Spey jet engines produce a combined total of 110,000 **horsepower** of force.

VALUE
The vehicle took about 100,000 man-hours of construction. To build it today would cost about £5.5 million.

13

SHINKAI 6500

The **Shinkai 6500** is a three-person deep sea **submersible** owned by the Japan Agency for Marine-Earth Science and Technology (JAMSTEC). On 11 August, 1989, it dived to a record-breaking depth of 6,527 metres in the Japan Trench off Sanriku. This was the deepest dive ever achieved by a manned submersible.

SPEED

Shinkai 6500's **maximum** speed is 2.5 **knots** (4.58 km/h) . This isn't fast, but the surveying work it carries out does not require it to travel at high speeds.

FEATURES

This submersible has a pressure-resistant shell made from super-strong **titanium**. It is equipped with the latest **navigation** and communications systems and carries two colour television cameras.

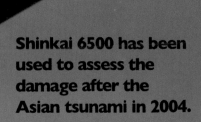

SIZE

Shinkai 6500 is 9.5 metres long and 2.7 metres wide – about the size of two four-wheel drive vehicles. This submersible weighs a massive 23 tonnes.

Shinkai 6500 has been used to assess the damage after the Asian tsunami in 2004.

POWER

The submersible is lowered to the seabed by its support vehicle Yokosuka. It then runs on batteries that last for about 12 hours.

VALUE

Shinkai 6500 cost about £53 million and each dive costs a further £16,000. However, the research it carries out, including earthquake prediction, could be priceless.

This submersible's shell is made of titanium.

EXTREME SCORES

Costly and heavy, but can go where no other submersible can reach.

SPEED 2/10

FEATURES 3/10

SIZE 4/10

POWER 3/10

VALUE 7/10

= TOTAL SCORE 19/50

V-22 OSPREY TILTROTOR

The V-22 is a dream come true for aircraft designers: it takes off and lands like a helicopter, but flies like a plane. It was developed for the US Marine Corps by Bell Helicopters, Textron and Boeing. It is the only US transport aircraft that has nuclear, **biological** and chemical protection.

SPEED

The V-22 has a top speed of 584 km/h – twice as fast as an ordinary helicopter.

FEATURES

The V-22 takes off, lands and hovers in helicopter mode with its **rotors** in vertical position.
In flight, its rotors are carried in the **horizontal** position.

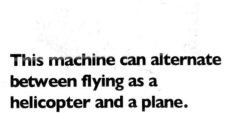

This machine can alternate between flying as a helicopter and a plane.

The V-22 can take off without a runway, just like a helicopter.

SIZE

This unique aircraft weighs around 13 tonnes and can carry a total load of 9,072 kg, including 24 marines.

POWER

The V-22 Osprey has two prop-rotors, each with a three-bladed **propeller**. Each propeller is driven by a turbo shaft engine capable of producing 6,150 **horsepower**.

VALUE

This aircraft has some amazing features, and it comes with the sky-high price tag of about £42.5 million.

The V-22 flies twice as far and twice as fast as a helicopter.

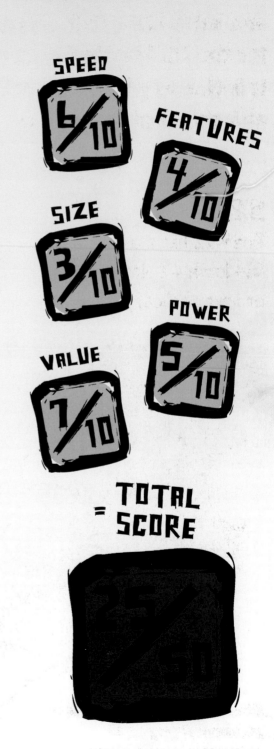

SPEED
6/10

FEATURES
4/10

SIZE
3/10

POWER
5/10

VALUE
7/10

= TOTAL SCORE

The **LCAC** (Landing Craft Air Cushion) is the only **amphibious** vehicle in our list. It was developed for the US Navy, and it is used to transport troops and equipment at high speeds. With this amazing hovercraft more than 70 per cent of the world's coastline is accessible, while only about 15 percent is accessible by conventional landing craft.

SPEED

Even fully-loaded, the LCAC has a top speed of more than 40 **knots** (74 km/h) – four times the speed of old fashioned landing craft.

FEATURES

This mighty hovercraft is flat-bottomed and is made from aluminium. It has a rubber air bladder and two **propellers**. Like an aircraft, it has a **cockpit** and is linked to air traffic control.

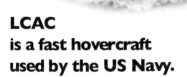

LCAC
is a fast hovercraft
used by the US Navy.

The LCAC can land in difficult conditions.

SIZE

This **amphibious** giant can carry a load of up to 61 tonnes and weighs more than 108 tonnes fully-loaded.

POWER

The LCAC Hovercraft uses four engines per vessel – two engines for lift and two engines for propulsion – providing a total of 16,000 **horsepower**.

VALUE

The LCAC carries a price tag of about £13.2 million. It was used to carry essential aid to victims of the Asian tsunami in 2004.

EXTREME SCORES

Can carry huge loads at high speed and can go where no other vehicle is able to go.

SPEED
4/10

FEATURES
4/10

SIZE
6/10

POWER
6/10

VALUE
6/10

= TOTAL SCORE
26/50

Thrust SSC (Supersonic Car) is the fastest and most powerful car ever built. British designer Richard Noble built the car to break the sound barrier over land. On 15 October, 1997, at Black Rock Desert, Nevada, US it reached the record-breaking speed of 1,232 km/h. It was driven by RAF pilot Andy Green.

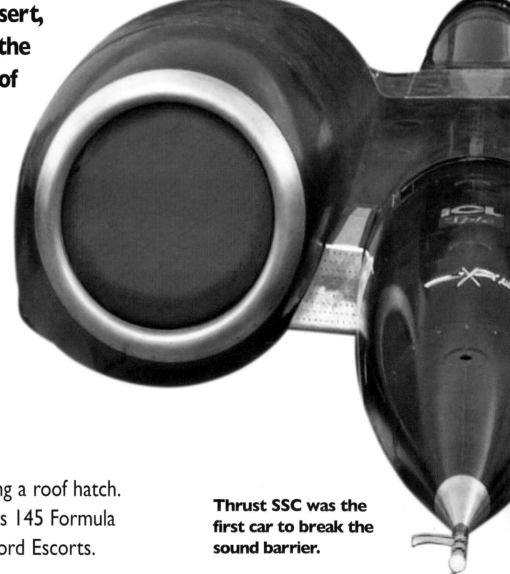

SPEED

Thrust's top speed is 1,367 km/h, and it can go from 0 to160 km/h in 4 seconds. It **accelerated** to 965 km/h in just 6 seconds.

FEATURES

The driver enters by opening a roof hatch. The vehicle is as powerful as 145 Formula One racing cars, or 1,000 Ford Escorts.

Thrust SSC was the first car to break the sound barrier.

SIZE

Thrust weighs 9 tonnes, and a parachute braking system is used to slow it down safely.

This record-breaking car draws crowds whenever it is on display.

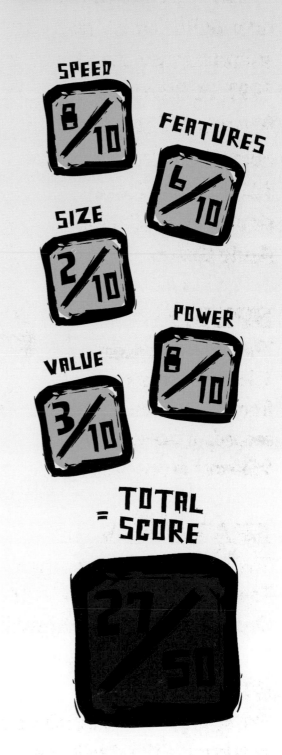

Supersonic speed and incredible power makes Thrust SSC a really extreme machine.

SPEED
8/10

FEATURES
6/10

SIZE
2/10

POWER
8/10

VALUE
3/10

= TOTAL SCORE

27/50

POWER

Its two Rolls Royce Spey jet engines produce a combined total of 110,000 **horsepower** of force.

VALUE

The vehicle took about 100,000 man-hours of construction. To build it today would cost about £5.5 million.

USS LOUISIANA

The USS Louisiana is the largest ballistic submarine ever built for the US Navy. It carries 24 Trident nuclear missiles that can be fired very quickly if needed. The submarine was named after the eighteenth state of the US, and built by General Dynamics' Electric Boat Division.

SPEED

This massive submarine patrols the sea at a speed of about 20 **knots** (37 km/h), fast enough to see off most enemy craft.

FEATURES

The USS Louisiana has one **propeller** and is powered by a nuclear reactor. It is capable of operating for more than 15 years before it needs refuelling.

SIZE

The USS Louisiana is 171 metres long, over 12 metres wide and weighs about 17,000 tonnes.

USS Louisiana was the last Trident submarine built.

USS Louisiana remains on active duty today.

POWER

The submarine's nuclear reactor is capable of generating a massive 60,000 **horsepower**.

VALUE

The USS Louisiana cost about £6.4 million to develop. Its main purpose is defence.

This nuclear-powered monster is the most extreme submarine ever built.

SPEED
3/10

FEATURES
6/10

SIZE
9/10

POWER
7/10

VALUE
4/10

= TOTAL SCORE
29/50

SPACESHIP ONE

SpaceShipOne is the world's first private manned spacecraft. It was developed by Burt Rutan and his aviation company, Scaled Composites. After take-off is carried to the edge of space by the aircraft White Knight. The spacecraft detaches, drops clear, and detonates its engine to continue. One day the technology might be used to fly tourists into space!

SPEED

SpaceShipOne has a peak speed of 4,023 km/h or about Mach 3. It was powered to this speed by 63-year-old test pilot Michael Melvill.

FEATURES

This craft is fuelled by a mix of laughing gas and rubber. In space, its wings are folded up to give a 'shuttlecock' effect which helps it to glide safely back to Earth.

SpaceShipOne is the first private manned spacecraft to fly at an altitude of over 97,000 metres.

SIZE

In rocket terms, this little craft is tiny. Made mostly from graphite, SpaceShipOne weighs just 1.08 tonnes and its wingspan is 5 metres.

POWER

SpaceShipOne's single rocket engine produces the equivalent of 96,973 **horsepower**.

VALUE

SpaceShipOne cost about £10.6 million, but won a £6 million prize established in 1996 to spur private space tourism. British airline entrepreneur Richard Branson also plans on using the technology to fly tourists into space as soon as 2007.

SpaceShipOne was released by the aircraft *White Knight* at a height of 14 kilometres.

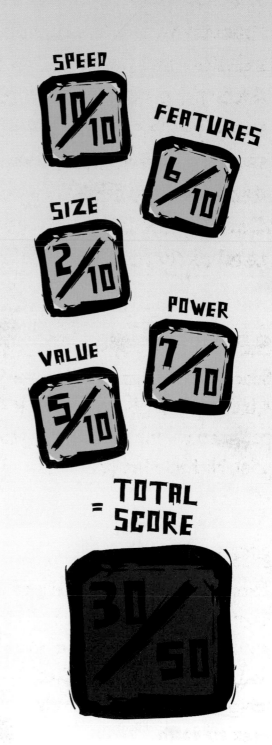

EXTREME SCORES

This extreme machine is a step ahead in the quest to conquer space travel.

SPEED
10/10

FEATURES
6/10

SIZE
2/10

POWER
7/10

VALUE
5/10

= TOTAL SCORE
30/50

The TGV Duplex is the world's fastest commercially-operated conventional train. It is operated by the French national railway company TGV (Train à Grand Vitesse). Nicknamed the workhorse of the TGV fleet, it operates mainly on the TGV Sud-Est line from Paris to Lyon.

SPEED

The name 'Train à Grande Vitesse' means high-speed train. TGV lived up to its name in 1990 when it reached speeds of 514 km/h.

FEATURES

This train is made from aluminium to keep the weight low. It has a central **cockpit** so it can be driven from the left or right.

SIZE

TGV Duplex is 200 metres long and weighs about 344 tonnes, and can carry up to 545 passengers.

POWER

TGV Duplex runs on electricity and has eight 3-phase synchronous AC traction motors, which generate about 12,000 **horsepower**.

EXTREME SCORES

The double-decker TGV Duplex can carry 545 passengers.

TGV Duplex is the world's fastest conventional train.

This extreme machine works hard, is super-fast and provides great comfort.

SPEED 6/10

FEATURES 7/10

SIZE 8/10

POWER 6/10

VALUE 9/10

= TOTAL SCORE

VALUE

The TGV Duplex cost more than £207 million. Its real value is that it lets more passengers travel on a busy route that could not have coped with extra trains.

LOCKHEED
SR-71

Affectionately known as the 'Blackbird', this plane was designed by a team led by Clarence 'Kelly' Johnson at the Lockheed company. It was developed as a long-range, advanced 'stealth' plane. Blackbird is no longer in service, but is still the fastest and highest-flying operational aircraft ever developed.

SPEED

In July 1976, SR-71 set a speed record of 3,529 km/h (Mach 3+) or more than three times the speed of sound.

FEATURES

The SR-71's airframe is made of **titanium**. It broke the speed record for its class and set an altitude record of 26,000 metres. No SR-71 was ever shot down or hit by enemy fire.

SIZE

This flying giant is 32.8 metres long with a 16.9 metre wingspan. Its loaded weight was 77,000 kgs.

Lockheed SR-71 is the world's fastest aircraft.

SR-71s have outrun more than 4,000 missiles.

POWER

Power was provided by two Pratt & Whitney J58 (JT11D-20A) high-bypass turbojets, capable of producing 160,000 **horsepower**.

VALUE

Each SR-71 cost around £13 million. The US Air Force retired its fleet in 1990 because of high operational costs. The planes were returned to service briefly in 1997.

EXTREME SCORES

This incredible flying machine is fast, powerful and effective, but in the end just too expensive.

SPEED
9/10

FEATURES
9/10

SIZE
5/10

POWER
8/10

VALUE
6/10

= TOTAL SCORE

ANTONOV AN-225

The An-225 Mriya ('dream') is the world's largest aircraft. Only one was ever made, to transport the Buran Space Shuttle, but the Russian space programme was abandoned after just one flight. The An-225 Mriya was designed and manufactured by OK Antonov ASTC in 1988.

SPEED
The An-225 is capable of flying at a top speed of almost 849 km/h, and can cruise at nearly 804 km/h.

FEATURES
Fully loaded, this plane could fly non-stop from New York to Los Angeles. Items too big to put inside can ride piggyback – objects up to 80 metres long!

The Antonov An-225 carries its loads in a 'piggyback' style!

SIZE
The An-225 is
84 metres long with an 88.4-metre wingspan, and weighs 410 tons. It has a **maximum** take-off weight of 600,000 kg.

The An-225 has a 32-wheel landing gear.

POWER

Power is provided by six ZMKB Progress Lotarev D-18T turbofan jets, each capable of pumping out 410,300 **horsepower**.

VALUE

This extreme machine cost about £160 million, yet was used to carry a shuttle into space just once!

Only one of these planes has ever been built, but there are plans to develop a second.

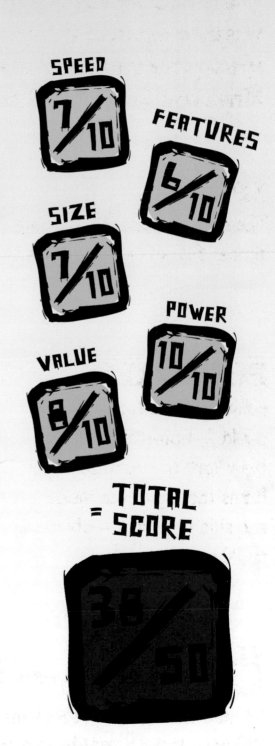

SPEED
7/10

FEATURES
6/10

SIZE
7/10

POWER
10/10

VALUE
8/10

= TOTAL SCORE

38/50

USS RONALD REAGAN

The USS Ronald Reagan aircraft carrier is the largest warship ever built. Named after America's 40th president, it carries a crew of more than 6,000 as well as more than 80 aircraft. It was built by the Newport News Shipbuilding and Dry Dock Company.

SPEED

The USS Ronald Reagan has a top speed of more than 30 **knots** and an almost unlimited range.

FEATURES

The CVN-76 was made using more than a billion parts from more than 3,000 suppliers. It can sail for more than 20 years before re-fuelling.

SIZE

This massive vessel is 332 metres long and weighs about 90,718 tonnes. The area of its flight deck is more than 18,000 m².

The USS Ronald Reagan is almost as long as the Empire State Building.

This massive vessel weighs more than all the other machines on our list put together. It is the ultimate extreme machine.

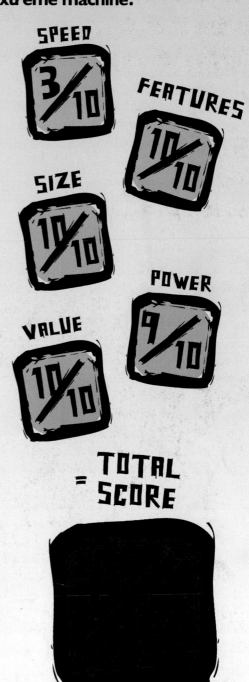

SPEED 3/10

FEATURES 10/10

SIZE 10/10

POWER 9/10

VALUE 10/10

= TOTAL SCORE

POWER

This huge ship is powered by two A4W **nuclear** reactors and four steam turbines, producing 260,000 **horsepower**!

This ship is sent all over the world for use in war and peacetime operations.

VALUE

The USS Ronald Reagan cost £2.5 billion to develop. It is expected to be in service for 50 years, so it could prove a sound long-term investment.

CLOSE
BUT NOT CLOSE ENOUGH

Choosing just ten extreme vehicles for this book was very difficult. Here are five amazing machines that didn't quite make the final list...

SPIRIT OF AUSTRALIA

This budget-priced hydroplane's world record has never been beaten. It was designed and built by Australian Ken Warby in his back yard for less than £5,300, and the engine was about £34 in an auction! At Blowering Dam, New South Wales on 8 October, 1978, Ken and 'Spirit' reached a top speed of 514 km/h. There have only been two official attempts to break Warby's record.

THE FA22 RAPTOR

This stealth jet was designed to be the 21st century's top fighter plane. Hydraulic arms launch air-to-air missiles from its internal weapons bays in less than a second. Built for the US Air Force by Lockheed Martin and Boeing, it cost about £137 million and has a top speed of over 1,931 km/h in super-cruise mode.

THE VOLVO EXTREME GRAVITY CAR

This aluminium and carbon fibre derby racer weighs about 16 kg and can hit nearly 56 km/h by the end of its 19.5m launch ramp. The lying-down driver position and **aerodynamic** shape help it to gain speed. It is steered with handlebars beneath the **fairing** and uses a rear wheel brake.

NUNA II

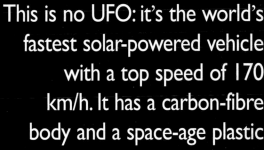

This is no UFO: it's the world's fastest solar-powered vehicle with a top speed of 170 km/h. It has a carbon-fibre body and a space-age plastic shell covered in solar cells. In October 2003 in Australia Nuna II won the World Solar Challenge, travelling 3,025 km in 31 hours 5 minutes. It was built and driven by students from Delft University, the Netherlands.

BIGFOOT

This massive vehicle is the biggest truck ever built. It is more than 3.66 metres tall with tyres that weigh 399 kg. Its 1,500 **horsepower** engine produces a top speed of more than 128 km/h. The Bigfoot series was developed by Bob Chandler and individual models can cost between £80,000 and £133,000.

NO. 10 SHINKAI 6500

		Extreme Scores	TOTAL SCORE
Country:	*Japan*		
Year:	*1989*	Speed	2
Manufacturer:	*JAMSTEC*	Features	3
No. of Passengers:	*3*	Size	4
Special Feature:	*Deepest dive ever*	Power	3
Cost:	*£53 million*	Value	7

TOTAL SCORE 19/50

NO. 9 V-22 OSPREY

		Extreme Scores	
Country:	*US*		
Year:	*1999*	Speed	6
Manufacturer:	*Bell Helicopters Textron*	Features	4
No. of Passengers:	*24*	Size	3
Special Feature:	*Plane and*	Power	5
	helicopter	Value	7
Cost:	*£42.5 million*		

TOTAL SCORE 25/50

NO. 8 LCAC HOVERCRAFT

		Extreme Scores	
Country:	*US*		
Year:	*1982*	Speed	4
Manufacturer:	*Textron Marine*	Features	4
	Systems/ Avondale Gulfport Marine	Size	6
No. of Passengers:	*24*	Power	6
Special Feature:	*Reaches 70% of coast*	Value	6
Cost:	*£13.2 million*		

TOTAL SCORE 26/50

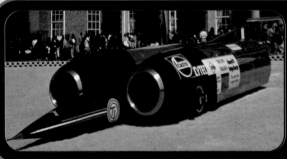

NO. 7 THRUST SSC

		Extreme Scores	
Country:	*UK*		
Year:	*1997*	Speed	8
Manufacturer:	*Richard Noble*	Features	6
	Partnership	Size	2
No. of Passengers:	*1*	Power	8
Special Feature:	*Fastest land speed*	Value	3
Cost:	*£5.3 million*		

TOTAL SCORE 27/50

NO. 6 USS LOUISANA

		Extreme Scores	
Country:	*US*		
Year:	*1997*	Speed	3
Manufacturer:	*General Dynamics*	Features	6
	Electric Boat Division	Size	9
No. of Passengers:	*154*	Power	7
Special Feature:	*60,000 horsepower*	Value	4
Cost:	*£6.4 million*		

TOTAL SCORE 29/50

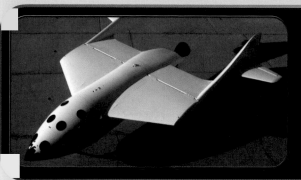

NO. 5 SPACESHIP ONE

Country:	US	**Extreme Scores**	
Year:	2003	Speed	10
Manufacturer:	Scaled Composites	Features	6
No. of Passengers:	3	Size	2
Special Feature:	First private	Power	7
	spacecraft	Value	5
Cost:	£10.6 million		

 TOTAL SCORE 30/50

NO. 4 TGV DUPLEX

Country:	France	**Extreme Scores**	
Year:	1997	Speed	6
Manufacturer:	GEC-Alsthom	Features	7
No. of Passengers:	545	Size	8
Special Feature:	Fastest train	Power	6
Cost:	£207 million	Value	9

TOTAL SCORE 36/50

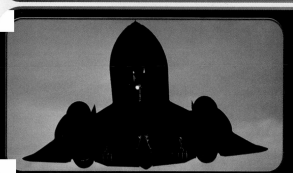

NO. 3 LOCKHEED SR-71

Country:	US	**Extreme Scores**	
Year:	1966	Speed	9
Manufacturer:	Lockheed Aircraft	Features	9
	Corporation	Size	5
No. of Passengers:	2	Power	8
Special Feature:	Fastest working plane	Value	6
Cost:	£13 million		

 TOTAL SCORE 37/50

NO. 2 ANTONOV AN-225

Country:	USSR	**Extreme Scores**	
Year:	1988	Speed	7
Manufacturer:	OK Antonov ASTC	Features	6
No. of Passengers:	7	Size	7
Special Feature:	Largest aircraft	Power	10
Cost:	£160 million	Value	8

 TOTAL SCORE 38/50

NO. 1 USS RONALD REAGAN

Country:	US	**Extreme Scores**	
Year:	2001	Speed	3
Manufacturer:	Newport News	Features	10
	Shipbuilding	Size	10
No. of Passengers:	6,000	Power	9
Special Feature:	Largest ever warship	Value	10
Cost:	£2.5 billion		

TOTAL SCORE 42/50

ACCELERATE Gather speed.

AERODYNAMIC Concerned with the way a vehicle moves through air or gas.

AMPHIBIOUS Able to be used both on land and water.

BIOLOGICAL Linked to the science of living things.

COCKPIT The part of a vehicle where the driver sits.

FAIRING A structure fitted round the outside of parts of a car or an aircraft to reduce drag.

HORIZONTAL Level or flat.

HORSEPOWER The amount of power a horse can exert, which is set at 550 foot-pounds per second or 74.5.7 watts.

KNOT A measurement of speed used for boats and aircraft, equal to one nautical mile (about 1.85 km) per hour.

MAXIMUM The greatest possible amount of anything.

NAVIGATION Planning a route and directing a ship or aircraft along it.

NUCLEAR ENERGY A type of energy produced by splitting an atom.

PROPELLER A shaft with spiral blades for driving an aircraft or vessel.

ROTOR A rotating part of a machine.

SUBMERSIBLE Able to be submerged or capable of operating under water.

SUPERSONIC Above the speed of sound or travelling faster than the speed of sound.

TITANIUM A strong white metal that resists corrosion.